The Limerickiad

The Limerickiad: volume III

from Byron to Baudelaire

Martin Rowson

Smokestack Books
PO Box 408, Middlesbrough TS5 6WA
e-mail: info@smokestack-books.co.uk
www.smokestack-books.co.uk

The Limerickiad: volume III
from Byron to Baudelaire
copyright 2013 by Martin Rowson
all rights reserved.

Cover illustration: Martin Rowson

Designed by Tony Marson (01773 836973)
Printed and bound by Martins the Printers Ltd,
Berwick-upon-Tweed.

Middlesbrough
moving forward

ISBN 978-0-9575747-0-0
Smokestack Books is represented
by Inpress Ltd

Thanks are due to the
Independent on Sunday,
where these poems first appeared.

Contents

Dedications require dedication,
So with this, my latest creation,
   The laurels are JOYCE's!
   She does my invoices.
Without her I'd need medication.

(While also, as oft is my manner,
Though I'd bet 50 quid to a tanner
   That by them it's unread,
   It's for ROSE and for FRED
And also my darling wife ANNA!)

Byron

If you think Lakeland Poets are chronic
Then steady yourself for a tonic
    For in Greece's environs
    You'll find that LORD BYRON's
Been out about being Byronic!

He was Romantic straight from the womb
And so kept a bear in his room
    At Trinity College,
    That fountain of knowledge
Where he drank like a fish, we presume.

For he'd boldly go further than Kirk'll,
Swimming Hellesponts just like a Turk'll
    (Though his club foot, alash*
    Meant that after the splash
He then swam around in a circle).

With his loose open shirt he's soon screwin'
Everyone on that old Road to Ruin!**
    But then, thus apparelled,
    He knocked out *CHILDE HAROLD*
And followed it up with *DON JUAN*!

*Both these variants apply, I insist,
  Because he was permanently pissed.

**Though it's rumoured he took off his vest
  When he finally sank to incest…

The Life of LORD BYRON doth show
How to be A Romantic, although
    He was said to be mad
    And equally bad
And likewise quite dangerous to know.

Nonetheless he earned massive acclaim as
CHILDE HAROLD came out (although Seamus
    Is a far better name
    For the rhyme I need – shame!*)
When he woke up next day he was famous.

This long poem first introduces
How the Byronic Hero produces,
    Through being outcast
    An extraordinarily vast
Volume of bodily juices

In readers, from which we conclude he
Was Romantic! Indeedy-doody!
    But how does one evince
    This status? Just mince
Across Europe while looking quite moody…

* And my scansion would light up the page
  If he'd left out that word *Pilgrimage*…

Poetry as She is Done
No. 12: "ASSONANCE"

"Byron with a Biro on his Burro"

Don Juan

In Lord Byron's poem *DON JUAN*
The hero starts off by pursuin'*
    A wild fling in Seville.
    The handsome young devil
Escapes on a ship. Trouble's brewin'.

After storms and a shipwreck, our JUAN
Sees his tutor and dog scoffed! The sun
    Warms the Isles of the Aegean
    While the anthropophagean
Crew are all dead! My, what fun!

Soon he's sold as a slave, is poor JUAN! Oh!
And then made to put on a bra! No!
    And thus in drag we go
    Through the seraglio!
A fan is soon hit by some guano!

This is just Canto V of *DON JUAN*,
An amount Byron thought was too few. On
    The whole with *DON JUAN*
    I'd prefer a haiku! One
Would then have much less stuff to chew on!

*If these rhymes all set off warning sirens,
  My rhyme scheme's just looser than Byron's…

The Death of Byron

When reviewing LORD BYRON's career,
Don't you think that it's frightfully queer
    To a very large part
    That his Life was his Art,
And his Poetry brings up the rear?

For who in their right minds would swear
That perusing, say *THE CORSAIR*
    Matches Freeing All Greece
    Or seeking release
Through incest with his sis? Go Compare!

But then, after years of applying
Himself to his life, he's then buying
    The farm! Dead and pongy
    In far Missolonghi
His Life's thus eclipsed by his dying!

For though critics may well have led one
To rate BYRON's odes have you read one?
    Thought not. But Romantics
    Are loved for their antics
And the best Romantic is a dead one!*

*Furthermore, to the average Greek,
  Though his body soon started to reek,
  He stuck to his Byronic riff.
  And thus made a good looking stiff…

Romanticism and Death

The death of LORD BYRON young poses
A problem. For how many doses
    Of blistering clap
    Must a Romantic chap
Contract to reach apotheosis?*

Or if you are lacking the gumption
For sex you can opt for Consumption!
    Go clean, quick or dirty,
    Just die under 30!
For otherwise there's an assumption

You'll sell out all that can be sold
That's Radical, Romantic, Bold!
    For who knows where you'll go
    If like WORDSWORTH & Co.
You ruin it all and grow old?

So if poets' bowels turn to jelly
At age 29, just say, 'Well, he
    Died young, which is queer
    But his brilliant career
Was Romantically short, just like SHELLEY!'

*Please do not cry out, 'Oh, you cynic!'
  But SCHUBERT, once spied at the clinic,
  Said to one of his homies, 'Yo brud!
  I'd rather be coughin' up blood
  Or dancin' around like St. Vitus
  When old an' wid osteoarthritis!
  But though 'avin the clap is the pits
  It's better than dyin' of squits.'

Shelley

Our next poet of call* is P. SHELLEY
Who gave being Romantic welly!
    Poetic, contrarian,
    Left-wing, vegetarian
And obviously destined for Hell, he

Was an atheist too! PERCY BYSSHE
Is every Romantic fan's wish!
    What's more, Lord a'Mercy,
    He died young, did PERCY,
By drowning and feeding the fish!

Yet though we, of the Poet, demand 'e 'as
The looks of ANTONIO BANDERAS
    And live as 'neath a curse
    Don't forget SHELLEY's verse!
Let's start off, then, with *OZYMANDIAS*.**

I met a chap who said 'Out there
Are two vast trunkless legs of stone, yeah?
    Being all that remain
    Of OZ save this refrain:
'Mighty! Look on my works and despair!'

*It's a pun! Do you get it? Heh heh!
  It's the way that I tell 'em, okay?

** Do I call this a rhyme? Since you ask
  It works like a treat said in Basque.

PERCY BYSSHE SHELLEY did pledge
'Poets are the unacknowledged leg-
    Islators of the World!'
    Once my toes have uncurled
I'll explain why my teeth are on edge.

SHELLEY argues (I'm not being snooty)
That bards should pass laws as they duty!
    Would it then be a crime
    To dodge metre and rhyme
Or break the laws of Truth and Beauty?

It gets worse. Though he hounded the pious
And exhibited clear left-wing-bias*
    Would PERC win applause
    If he brought in new laws
To enforce weeping for ADONIAS?

'Hail to thee, blithe spirit!' he wrought.
'Bird thou never wert!' Who'd have thought?
    If it's not a skylark,
    What is it? A shark?!
The thing wouldn't stand up in court!

*Shelley laid into kings with aplomb! He
  Was really a prototype Commie!

The Mask of Anarchy

As I lay asleep in Italy
There came a voice over the sea
    Which led me from thence
    To 200 years hence
To walk in dreams of Po-e-sy!

I met MURDOCH on the way! Yuck!
Behind him vile hacks raked up muck
    So repellent, I swore,
    They defied metaphor!*
Behind them, continuing to suck,

Stood Greed, Office, POWER, all clammerin'
For favour; each looked like DAVE CAMERON
    (With a snapped wooden leg
    Which looked like NICK CLEGG)
While behind him slouched GEORGE OSBORNE, hammerin'

The Poor! And behind him, I knew,
The Banks lurked, preparing to spew
    Forth poison, like flies!
    So like LIONS, please rise:
Ye are many – and they are few!

*Space forbids me from mentioning a stable
  Filled with dung, which looked just like VINCE CABLE!
  Or gruel that had spilled down a stove
  To rust it; it looked just like GOVE;
  Or a venomous spider which tickles
  As its web traps you – looks just like PICKLES;
  And let's not forget that J HUNT
  Who looks like a right stuck-up...

The Death of Shelley

As we now bid a sad bon voyage
To SHELLEY's thin pale visage
    Was he *ODE TO A LARK*
    Or JOHN COOPER CLARKE?
We should now be told, by and large.

See, when poets knock out their screeds,
Some write about something which bleeds
    (Like macho TED HUGHES)
    While some skip with the Muse.
So are poets manly, or weeds?

While Shelley hymned freedom for hours
He's then writing verse to wild flowers!
    Hello trees, hello clouds?
    Or whipping up crowds?
Make your mind up on who this empowers!

For though he came on Us and Them,
He wrote cissy poems! (Hem hem!)
    The question's profound:
    If he hadn't have drowned
Do you think he'd have voted Lib Dem?*

*You can see all the odes SHELLEY made,
 But not one single barricade...

Mary Shelley

We're now used to SHELLEY complaining
About Tyrants, but it's worth explaining
    That his second wife MARY
    Was terribly scary,
Especially when it was raining!

Was she psychotic*? Did she achieve a
Reputation with a cleaver
    And collect heads in brine?
    No. She wrote *FRANKENSTEIN*
On holiday near to Geneva.

We all know the plot. MARY picked a
Mad scientist name of VICTOR;
    Made a man out of bodies
    Who finds out who God is
Reading Miltonic *Obiter Dicta*

The whole thing is Romantic tosh
With a monster who goes bish bash bosh,
    Though unlike SHELLEY's odes
    It's been made into loads
Of x-rated horror films! Gosh!**

*Consider the murderous antics
  Of LAMB's sister and other Romantics.

**Though they've tried, screenwriters have found
  Too few chills in *PROMETHEUS UNBOUND.*

Keats

Nobody really competes
With the way the Grim Reaper depletes
    The ranks of young poets
    And therefore we know it's
Time to get stuck into KEATS!

It's terribly easy to scoff,
With SHELLEY & BYRON knocked off
    Drowned/fighting Turks
    Whereas with KEATS, the berk's
Taken before with a cough.

But that is to make the assumption
That Keats was a weed, lacking gumption.
    Did you not learn in school
    It's incredibly cool
And Romantic to die of consumption?

So forget all those poems forlorn;
KEATS had more in common with porn!
    What his lifespan might lack!
    He made up in the sack!
And that's how he'd get FANNY BRAWN(E)*

*Keats kept *schtum* on this, fearing harassment.
 It's in RICK's *KEATS & EMBARRASSMENT*.

Having reached our review of JOHN KEATS
This comprehensively completes
    The Romantic poets
    (And these reviews show it's
Poems that still count, not Tweets!)

Though he tried many poetic modes
Keats is best known for his ODES:
    Just watch how he churns
    Out stuff about urns*
And Autumn and things. He wrote loads!

And no one could really dispute he
Knew that his Romantic duty
    Was simply to show
    That all we need to know
Is that Beauty is Truth, and Truth Beauty!

And if you should read him with glumness,
Subject to a strange, drowsy numbness
    As if hemlock you'd drunk...
    You philistine punk!
This merely points out your own dumbness!

*Though these days the average Greek yearns
  To earn enough to afford urns!

Ode to Autumn

'Season misty and fruitily mellow;
Chum of sun, now a deepening yellow;
    Swelling gourds, plumping nuts
    And conspiring at gluts
Of honey as clammy as jello!

Who hath not seen thee oft mid thy store?
Poppy-fumed, on the granary floor?
    Or thinking of boozing
    By a cider-press oozing
Hours by hours (*think we all know the score*).

Where are the songs of Spring? Where they?
While barred clouds bloom, the soft-dying day
    With a rosy hued touch
    (*Is this getting too much?*
If it's over the top please do say).

Gnats sink as the wind lives or dies;
Grown up lambs bleat while in a hedge lies
    Crickets. Near trebling soft,
    A redbreast, in a croft;
While swallows all tweet in the skies!'*

*Every toe dipped in bliss needs a splinter,
 So here's mine: Sod this lark! Roll on winter!!

"Keats & Embarrassment"

La Belle Dame sans Merci

Ere moving on, it must be said
That KEATS has been often misread;
    He's a hot blooded fella
    And wrote in *ISABELLA*
About BASIL, on pot, giving head!

In *THE EVE OF ST. AGNES* the weather
Is cold, but the dreams are hot! Clever
    Folk get his thrust:
    That it's not simply just
Things of beauty that are joys for ever!*

And here is the proof KEATS was mucky:
Out with SHELLEY one night he got lucky,
    Although after he scored
    He loudly deplored
The way his girl said, 'Five bob, ducky!'

'Palely loitering in this whorehouse, Percy,'
Cried KEATS, 'like hogs transformed by CIRCE,
    We may pay just tanners,
    But what of good manners?'
Perc replied, 'That's La Belle Dame sans Merci!'**

*This version's not widespread, but hey!
  I'll prove all when I read KEATS one day!

**With his health issues KEATS soon forgot
  How that evening he caught elfin grot.

Nineteenth Century Philosphers

In this Limerickian depiction
I appear to have ill-served non-fiction
    Of the Romantic Age.
    Oh, get back in your cage!
Here's ten sages, without interdiction:

For starters, the post-Kantian FICHTE
Had German Philosophy licked
    (And would oft share a bagel
    With SCHELLING and HEGEL)
But be patient. I will not restrict

This list to philosophers. DARWIN
(ERASMUS, that is) was quite charmin'
    And no one was groovier
    Than BUFFON, save CUVIER,
And HUNTER the surgeon disarmin';

DALTON teased sunlight from a cucumber*;
MALTHUS thought populations encumber
    The Earth. That's nine. Tenth? Um...
    Ah! JEREMY BENTHAM!
The most happiness for the most number!**

*That's not true, though the smells were less beastly
 From his lab than from that of J. PRIESTLY.

**This phrase's contraction's contrarian,
 But sod it! It's Utilitarian!

The German Romantics

With KEATS, SHELLEY & BYRON all dead
Romanticism now fled
    Back across the North Sea
    To – gulp! – Germany
Where it all started off. For tis said

When he knocked off *THE SORROWS OF WERTHER*
It did not for a second occur ter
    That sad story's creator
    That 40 years later
They'd still be *Sturm und Drang* (so claimed GOETHE)*,

When you'd think by now they'd had their filla
The musings of SCHLEGAL and SCHILLER
    Or th'alienated pose o'
    Each bloody composer
Like SCHUBERT, syphilitic pillar

Of the German Romantics! We need a
Martian** perspective, dear reader,
    A little green chap
    Who'd cut through the crap:
'Cheer up earthling! Take me to your lieder!'

*He'd been writing *FAUST* and being arty
  Since the time of the Boston Tea Party.

**GOETHE wouldn't approve: then again
  I don't think that he'd read much CRAIG RAINE.

Bulwer-Lytton

Just about everybody was smitten
With The Romantics, and yet, in Britain
    One must feel somewhat vexed
    That they thought what came next
Was as good! Alas ED.BULWER-LYTTON

Wrote novels we now see as kittin'
Out Lit's dainty hand like a mitten!
    That is: woolly & loose –
    And to think, some poor goose
Lost its feathers to write down this shit! In

THE LAST DAYS OF POMPEII, ED's a fright
But they loved it!* And this was despite
    His dull leaden prose
    Which in *PAUL CLIFFORD* shows
With 'It was a dark and stormy night' –

The worst opening line ever written,
With no hope of line 2 him acquittin':**
    'The rain fell in torrents'.
    Well it ain't D. H. LAWRENCE,
So I think we'll move on from LORD LYTTON!***

* Weirdly his books, like *RIENZI,*
  Drove his readership into a frenzy.

** Don't blame me! Cast aside aspersion!
  I just ape LYTTON's way with inversion!

*** As a novelist he's down in steerage,
    But he sold, so moved up to the peerage!

Pushkin

While Britain was waiting for DICKENS
We mustn't ignore the rich pickin's
    To be found off in Russia!
    Behold PUSHKIN usher
In Russian Lit! How the pulse quickens!

Though not cut out to knock off a thriller*
He still sighed 'As I clutch at this quill a
    Desire to begin
    On *EUGEN ONEGIN***
Or finish *RUSLAN AND LUDMILLA*

Or spark my land's literary renewal
Is thwarted! Why is life so cruel
    That I keep on puddin' off
    Writing *BORIS GODUNOV*
When soon I'll get killed in a duel?

Cos I'm Russian! And gloomy! My soul
Is moody and dark on the whole,
    And racked with despair
    But Hey! Do I care?
I can leave all the jokes to GOGOL'

*If he'd penned crime fiction, I attest,
  Hard boiled might describe *THE STONE GUEST*...

**If these rhymes cause you some consternation
  They're obviously lost in translation!

The American Novel

Russian lit is great, though I confess
There's other Lit too! Go on! Guess!
 From around 1820
 Where d'you think there was plenty
Of Lit sloshing round? The US!

This was no surprise in this young nation.
Their Independence Declaration
 Was wholly engrossin'
 While SUSANNA ROWSON*
Wrote better than any damned Haitian!**

CHARLOTTE TEMPLE topped best seller lists
For decades, but then Nativists
 Like WASHINGTON IRVING
 In fashions unnerving
Wrote so much they sprained both their wrists!

And then there's that tale of a hunk
Fighting Indians through woods prowled by skunk,
 Though what fatally weakens
 That book on Mohicans
Is they're now the haircut on a punk.***

*Just watch it! I won't have you lousin'
 Up my given name saying 'ROWSON'!

**Though it's said none wrote haikus as pure
  As MONSIEUR TOUSSAINT L'OUVERTURE...

*** Just as HAWKEYE was ace with a bullet
   FENIMORE COOPER favoured the mullet...

French Literature

1830s. In Paris STENDHAL
Dodged mobs to a café. 'Look pal,
    No reader cried "Phwooar!"
    As they read *DE L'AMOUR*,
Nor was there a hint of *scandale**

In my next book *LE ROUGE ET LE NOIR*!
You could read it aloud to the choir
    Over in Notre Dame!'
    But a comforting arm
Now silenced STENDHAL. 'Listen Squire,'

Said BALZAC, 'please try this solution:
French books don't mean moral pollution!
    My *COMEDIE HUMAINE*
    All pure life doth contain...'
But S. broke in: 'Watch out! Revolution!!

The mob's risen! The times are unstable!
We'd best both hide under this table!
    But first, BALZAC, you go
    And tell VICTOR HUGO
To stop looking so miserable!'*

*If this cheap rhyme just fails to amaze
  Remember he speaks e*n français*...

** And if this rhyme tempts you to yawn
  HUGO'd been in there drinking since dawn.

Notre Dame de Paris

QUASIMODO just wanted to marry
(In HUGO's *NOTRE-DAME DE PARIS*)
    The fair ESMERALDA
    Although he repelled 'er
Being so mingin' he would embarrass*

The mingin'est minger! His hunch
Made passers-by bring up their lunch
    While his face was so foul
    It would loosen your bowel…
And yet, when it came to the crunch

He saved ESMERALDA, was brave
And noble, and as she once gave
    Him water to swallow
    After he'd killed FROLLO,
QUAS joined poor hanged ES in her grave!**

Yet like any Parisian chef
He never drew one sober breath!
    So what was the tipple
    Of this tragic cripple?
It's clear! It's the Bells made him deaf!!***

*Quite frankly you should have been spared
  This rhyme scheme. The whole thing is *merde*!

**This skimped plot don't make me no crook!
  If you want to know more, read the book!

*** A cathedral homed QUAS. In a house
  He'd clearly have drunk Famous Grouse…

Dickens

Do you all recall, in 2012
The Olympics? Those memories shelve
    For here we're much keener re:
    DICKENS' bicentenary
So into his work we'll now delve

From *BOZ* to *OUR MUTUAL FRIEND*,
Where one rule will never unbend!
    When a young nipper sickens
    Depend upon DICKENS
To make us all blub by the end!

And TV Executives know –
Just like if it's Christmas there's snow –
    That the Nation's pulse quickens
    At the thoughts of CHARLES DICKENS
As the BBC1 ratings show!

So in spite of the ludicrous plots
And a mawkishness that quickly clots
    And cloys as it thickens
    When bloody CHARLES DICKENS
Says 'Want any more?' we cry 'Lots!!'

Sketches by Boz

He wellied out books by the doz.,
Did DICKENS, and this woz becoz
    'E done proper! 'E'd start
    Wiv BEGINNINGS, an art
We shall ape, so here's *SKETCHES BY BOZ*!

That's enough. Afterwards he released a
Much better book I am pleased ter
    Say, and t'ain't rude,
    But to reach 'EDWIN DROOD'
We must speed up or be here till Easter!

Which isn't to say that the book stank
(Though the sketches, in truth, are by CRUIKSHANK)
    Yet the flames of hope gutter
    For each whimsical nutter –
Not to mention each scold, drunk, saint, schnook, crank

And mawkish old twerp – who adorned
His later books herein gets spawned.
    For look! Up there! Perchin'!
    Sweet Christ! It's an urchin!!
Don't say that you haven't been warned.

The Posthumous Papers of the Pickwick Club

DICKENS' next hit, *PICKWICK PAPERS*
Relates the eponymous capers
 Of portly old PICKWICK
 Whose girth needs a triptych
To fit him all in: ask his drapers.

As he views the world PICKWICK's eyes wrinkle
And he isn't averse to what drink'll
 Do when drunk deeply
 In coaching inns cheaply
Booked for the night by NAT TWINKLE

And SNODGRASS and TUPMAN (all single)
Who then all eternally mingle
 With WHIMSICAL COVES
 Who turn up in droves
Again and again, like ALF JINGLE

Or sleepy FAT BOY or SAM WELLER
(Who aphorizes *a capella*)
 Or the WARDLES who – Hell! –
 Live at Dingley Dell!!
Lock the whole sodding lot in a cellar!*

*Though a doctor would view this whole frolic
 As pathology, not just bucolic:
  Sleep apnoea; sweats;
  O.C.D and Tourette's
 With the rest obese and alcoholic!!

Oliver Twist

The poor orphan OLIVER TWIST
Said 'Please sir, I want some more!' Hissed
    The beadle named BUMBLE,
    'I'll teach you to grumble!'
He gets more than a slap on a wrist.

Continually underfed
To London young OLLIE's soon fled
    Where the ARTFUL DODGER
    Helps him be the lodger
Of FAGIN* (of whom it is said –

Though DICKENS was this social critic
Who paints the slums' air as mephitic,
    He gives Hope to poor tykes
    If not to BILL SIKES –
Yet F's portrayal's anti-semitic).

Through the plot's twists and turns how one longs
For the righting of all the cruel wrongs
    That make OLLIE forlorn
    Phew! Turns out he's well born!
All ends well**. I prefer it with songs…

*They live in a room in a rookery
 And earn a mean crust out of crookery...

**Chuck's sympathies seem quite distorted
  For his Lowlifes: THE DODGER's transported;
  BUMBLE ends in the workhouse – well fancy!
  FAGIN's hanged and BILL SIKES murders NANCY.

Nicholas Nickleby

There was a young NICK name of NICKLEBY
Who found out quite soon Fate can fickle be
    When RALPH his cruel uncle
    Cackled 'That punk'll
Now find out what kind of prick I'll be!'

Nick meets SMIKE at Dotheboys Hall
(Which OFSTED would judge 'Failing School')
    And beats WACKFORD SQUEERS,*
    The head, to loud cheers!
Both NICK and SMIKE flee! That's not all.

NICK spies MADDIE BRAY. 'Soon that chick'll be –
After many plot twists – Mrs NICKLEBY!'
    Though the bint nearly weds
    GRIDE – to clear her Dad's debts!**
But in the end that's where NICK's dick'll be.

The plots twist and sting like an ickle bee,
Though with RALPH's plottings just think how sick he'll be –
    When SMIKE dies – how sad! –
    Turns out RALPH was his Dad!!
Tops himself! Happy ending for NICKLEBY!

*Apart from C. Dickens what hack would
 Dare call a headmaster WACKFORD?

**I don't care if this weak rhyme enrages –
 I'm précising 900 pages!

The Old Curiosity Shop

In *THE OLD CURIOSITY SHOP*
They'll probably sell you a mop
    So that when you hear tell
    Of poor LITTLE NELL
You can mop up your tears as they drop!

For the cruel crippled dwarf DANIEL QUILP
Beats NELL's grandad at cards! Wiv a yilp*
    When he sees wot vey'd lorst
    Gramps & LITTLE NELL crorssed
The country to flee, beyond 'ilp!

The shop is now QUILP's, the monstrosity,
Though he no longer stocks Curiosity
    Save for his use, the spiv!
    'Does LITTLE NELL live?'
The Readers cry with furiosity!

She don't!!! I don't know about you
Ignore these red eyes – it's the flu –
    But – excuse me – Gulp! – If…
    It's no use… Sob!! Sniff!!
Wha-aaa-aaa-aaa-aaa!!Boo Hoo Hoo!!!**

*If you don't like these rhymes please don't mock me:
  These coves speak Dickensian Cockney.

**Because I'm a feeble old sniveller
  I've ignored KIT, the GENT and DICK SWIVELLER…

Barnaby Rudge

We next come to *BARNABY RUDGE*
Whose hero's a simpleton. Smudge
    That tear away! Read
    The Gordon Riots lead
To him near getting' 'anged! But begrudge

Me not if I cry – I'm no drudge!
Do you honestly want me to trudge
    Through the Byzantine plot
    (Which *I've mostly forgot)*
Of the story of *BARNABY RUDGE*?*

Though I might just concede, at a nudge
In this tale where we're called on to judge
    Politicians as craven
    That GRIP the tame raven
Is a good bit in *BARNABY RUDGE.*

But on the whole it's hard to budge
The thought that in *BARNABY RUDGE*
    When riots are Dickensian
    They're less Albigensian
And as cozy as clotted cream fudge...

*I've left out JOE, STAGG, HAREDALE, VARDEN
 And TAPPERTIT too. Beg yer pardon.

Martin Chuzzlewit

The eponymous cove MARTIN CHUZZLEWIT
Finds life is an unending puzzle. It
    Transpires his grandad
    Disinherits the lad
Cos he wants to wed MARY and nuzzle tit*.

SETH PECKSNIFF's morality wuzzle shit*
And hypocrisy pure, though no fuzz'll fit*
    Him up, and the onus
    Of crime falls on JONUS
A two-timing, murderous CHUZZLEWIT.

Then the novelist of *MARTIN CHUZZLEWIT*
Thinks a bit to mock our Yankee cuz'll fit
    In here – though it fails
    And trashed US sales
When he wrote how Americans huzzle it*.

SARAH GAMP the drunk nurse sure can guzzle it,
And MARY becomes Mrs CHUZZLEWIT
    And gramps faked the tiff
    To see off PECKSNIFF!
If this book was a dog you would muzzle it.

*These rhymes would be much better if
 The hero had been called John Smith.

Dombey and Son

The wife of the cold merchant DOMBEY
Dies! And thus without a Mom be
    Her poor newborn son
    And a girl Dad'll shun
But she doesn't turn into a zombie.*

The eponymous son of old DOMBEY
Aged 6 goes to Brighton. The Prom be
    No place for such youth
    Who then snuffs it! In truth
He doesn't turn into a zombie.*

Thereafter the new Mrs Dombey
Gets off with CARKER like a bomb! He
    Falls under a train!
    So here's Death once again
But HE doesn't turn into a zombie!*

When WALTER, friend of young Miss DOMBEY,
Is reportedly drowned, with aplomb he
    Comes back from the dead
    Though it has to be said
Even HE isn't really a zombie!*

*With a book with folk called TOOTS and TOODLES
 How can I get it in your noodles
 That sometimes, with limericks, you figure
 That certain rhymes are *de rigeur*?

David Copperfield

The widowed mum of DAVID COPPERFIELD
Weds MURDSTONE and so her vows stop her shield
    Her son from M's wrath!
    Then she dies! Davey's off
To a factory to earn a proper yield.

But MICAWBER*, in debt, comes a cropper! Steeled
To trudge through Kent, DAVE, in a flop appealed
    To Aunt BETSEY TROTWOOD**
    But years later what should
We make of the plot? 'Oh Lor'! Stop 'er!' squealed

THE PEGGOTTYS! Niece EM'LY'd swap a field
For DAVE's schoolchum STEERFORTH, a fop, a heel'd
    Be the novel's main creep
    If it weren't for U. HEEP
'Oo's 'umble (but best call a copper). Wield

Thy scythe, Death! Steerforth's ship, now pop a keel!
HAM (Emily's truelove), drown! Stop a meal
    For Dave's wet wife DORA
    Who now goes before!*** A-
GNES weds DAVE, who can now cop a feel…

* 'Spend not more than you earn!' without cease
  He'd say, but not do. Bit like Greece…

** She seems like a mean, dry old stick,
  But is comforted by MR. DICK!

*** Nurse PEGGOTTY's love, willing BARKISS
  Ends up as a very rich carcase…

Bleak House

London's fog (thick enough now to slice)
Ain't the only thing round 'ere's not nice
    When Lawyers glance a fee
    In Courts of Chancery
Hearing JARNDYCE v JARNDYCE!

In the sub-plots* the heroine ESTHER
Is told that her guardian confessed a
    Fondness, though pox
    Spoiled her looks, and that shocks
MR GUPPY, who'd mentally undressed 'er.

Then TULKINGHORN, top brief (and bent)
Squeezed LA DEDLOCK (whose youth was mis-spent);
    Meanwhile SMALLWEED disgusts;
    KROOK spontaneously combusts
And the court case costs every last cent!

But worst of all JOE'S dead! Dear me!
The crossing sweep 'moved on', you see,
    So all sob, but would lawyers
    Completely destroy us
If we simply had No Win, No Fee?!?'

*If I 'ad five bob for each subplot
 I'd 'ave more than the lawyers 'ave got!

Hard Times

In Coketown* in Dickens' *HARD TIMES*
The soot from the fact'ries begrimes
    The lot, plus the mind
    Of THOMAS GRADGRIND
Whose Utilitarian** crimes

Include him continuing to force
A small girl to define a horse!
    (It's a quadruped
    And gramnivorous. Ed.)
But Facts ain't the whole Truth, of course!

The poor millhand STEPHEN BLACKPOOL
Never even got close to a school.
    His life's bleak & drab,
    And what's worse he's a scab!
Then he falls down a mine, the old fool.

G's son's a thief; girl's an old maid;
The bosses doomed; hands underpaid;
    But if you think life's rough
    For these poor people, tough!
That's the price we all pay for Free Trade!!

*If the novel were happening today
  The location would move to LA!

**Though nobody said, with a thrill,
  'There's trooble oop JOHN STUART MILL!'

Little Dorritt

We all think that we should abhor it,
But with Debt there's just one thing for it
    To the Marshalsea Gaol –
    Which though beyond the pale
Has been home for years to LITTLE DORRITT!

Then with ARTHUR CLENNAM's intrusion
There's hope he might find a solution
    To old DORRITT's debt
    (Don't break out in a sweat)
At the Office of Circumlocution!

But the plot puts up many a hurdle:
Murd'rous Frenchies; the bent banker MERDLE
    And an airhead called FLORA.
    ART did once adore 'er,
Yet the milk of man's kindness doth curdle.

By the end both our heroes are rich
And ARTHUR's False Mum, who's a bitch,
    Is struck down by a stroke!
    What a wonderful joke
If that struck Ratings Agency FITCH!*

*See? You may think my verse is inept
  But I've brought the whole thing back to Debt!!

A Tale of Two Cities

'Twas the best of times – also the worst,
With Dr. MANETTE for years cursed
    Cobbling in The Bastille
    With no chance of appeal
'Til 'Recalled to Life'. Now we're immersed

In the worst of times (also the best).
At his trial DARNAY's jury's impressed
    He's the bleeding dead spit
    For CARTON, a git,
And they both love M's girl! Who'da guessed?

So. It was the best *and* worst of times
When D's uncle EVREMONDE's crimes
    Make MADAME DEFARGE,
    Comme la mer sur la plage
Lead the mob to rise up! The knell chimes

For the NOBS! This means DARNAY! Oh Lor'!
But as guillotines dribble with gore
    CARTON finds grace
    When he takes DARNAY's place,
Which is better than he'd done before* **

*Far far better, actually, as
  The rest he went after to was!

** I've left out MISS PROSS, JARVIS LORRY,
  JERRY CRUNCHER and GASPARD too. Sorry.

Great Expectations

By his family's graveside young PIP
Meets a convict escaped from a ship!
      'If you don't want to die
      You shall fetch me some pie!'
Says the lag, so PIP does! Blinking flip!

Miss HAVERSHAM, local rich nutter,
Has a house filled with dust, spite & clutter.
      Her adoptee ESTELLE
      Views PIP like a bad smell,
Worse than Miss H's old bridal schmutter!

Then suddenly PIP becomes rich!
Puts this down to the crazy old bitch
      So preens round like a ponce! Er…
      The convict's his sponsor!
(The old bugger's name is MAGWITCH.)

The adventures on which PIP embarks
Conclude when her dress catches sparks!
      Miss H gets immolated!
      JOE GARGERY stated
'What larks, eh, young PIP lad? What larks!'

Our Mutual Friend

At the start of *OUR MUTUAL FRIEND*
GAFFER HEXAM rows right round the bend
    Of that old River Thames
    Whose dark water claims
JOHN HARMON! (Disbelief suspend!)

J.'s the heir to a miser who's just
Croaked, so his vast piles of dust
    Go instead to the BOFFINS
    Whose gaucheness earns scoffins
From Toffs (who are nonetheless bust).

The kind BOFFINS take in young BELLA
Affianced (unseen) to the drowned fella.
    Plus JOHN ROKESMITH, who saw
    HARMON's corpse, and what's more,
You start to feel like Helen Keller

Trying to work out who's who, and who's found
The latest will; who's loved; who's drowned;
    Till you wish all the men*
    (Plus of course JENNY WREN)
Had been buried beneath that dust mound...

*That's HARMON/ROKESMITH, HEADSTONE, WEGG,
 RIDERHOOD and WEGG's bloody PEGLEG...

The Mystery of Edwin Drood

THE MYSTERY OF EDWIN DROOD
With Mystery's fully imbued
   'Cos the book is UNFINISHED
   Which frankly diminished
The ways that the plot lines conclude.

We know there's this weed EDWIN DROOD
Whose choirmaster uncle (who's stewed
   In dope) lusts for ROSA,
   ED's girl, which will pose a
Problem, as will EDWIN's feud

With NEVILLE, whose heart is now glued
To ROSA too! Who'll get pursued
   For ED's MURDER?! Vexed,
   Readers begged, 'What comes next??!'*
I believe DICKENS planned to play rude:

So ROSA & NEVILLE get screwed
By CRISPARKLE, vicar and dude,
   While UNCLE gets ripped
   To his tits in the crypt
And they all dance around in the nude!

*With the thoroughness of any creditor
 Death was DICKENS' last editor,
 Though with this plot, and old twerps called DURDLES
 Dropping dead was the least of Chuck's hurdles...

A Christmas Carol

We think 'Panama' when we hear 'Isthmus'
And 'Bellyache' when we read 'Bismuths',
    And stagecoaches in drifts
    And ghosts in pale shifts
Mean DICKENS, which therefore means 'Christmas'!!!

He wrote five Christmas novellas (four
Of which we can safely ignore
    Without scraping the barrel).
    In *A CHRISTMAS CAROL*
When SCROOGE hears a knock on the door,

Cos he treats his staff like a dictator*,
He'll hear MARLEY'S GHOST** tell him 'Later
    You will see three more spooks!!'
    And each one rebukes
This miserable old wealth creator!***

The visits leave SCROOGE quite undone,
So he saves TINY TIM and has fun
    Because seen through the prism
    Of ghosts, Thatcherism
Is crap! Bless us all, everyone!

*It's quite clear from what's writ on the page
  You can't live on the minimum wage...

**For years SCROOGE had done the same job
  As MARLEY – that's JACOB, not BOB.

*** If the plot requires more subtle shading
  View these visits as insider trading!

Dickens and Sentimentality

And so, we now finish with DICKENS,
With each plot that tortuously thickens
    And each hero searchin'
    For some wheezing Urchin
Who thereafter rapidly sickens

And DIES! And we're through with the Misers
On whose knees, 'midst many surprises,
    The aforementioned Urchin
    May well end up perchin'
While the Miser's financial advisers

Will end – though they're 'umble – in gutters!
Plus, we're finished with all of those nutters,
    Those eccentrics whose looks
    You'll just find in BOOKS!
And although every Heart of Stone flutters

And tears well up cos – yep, you've guessed..
We're each, everyone of us, Blessed,
    We're sick of morality
    And sentimentality!!!!
Phew! Thank God I've got that off my chest!

Edward Lear

In that bicentennial year
Of DICKENS, dear reader, while we're
    On the subject, please let
    Us all not forget
The same applied to EDWARD LEAR!

(Though in Eng. Lit, sweet reader, I fear
You must make sure you get the right LEAR:
    One writes nonsense verses;
    The other disperses
His land to his daughters. All clear?)

And though LEAR was decidedly queer
He invented the Limerick – so dear
    To my heart, for this form
    Helps me eat and keep warm!
Let's write one about him right here!

'When that runcible fellow called LEAR
Repeatedly sucked his own ear
    He cried, "Bingly-bongly!"
    Increasingly strongly
And did so throughout his career!'

Edgar Allen Poe

This page I had hoped to explore
EDGAR ALLEN POE's work, that dark lore
    The Horror & Mystery
    And Weird Occult History
But I heard something say 'Nevermore'.

I would speak of the hood and the claw,
How the Tell-Tale Heart beats 'neath the floor,
    Of Death and the Grave an'
    A bloody great raven
Interrupted and cawed 'Nevermore'.

On *THE PIT AND THE PENDULUM'S* gore,
Or the murders wrought in the Rue Mor-
    Gue, I'd be heard
    But that sodding black bird
Drowned my words out with each 'Nevermore'!

So I lunged at the git with a saw!
And screamed, 'You're becoming a bore!'
    Now I'll just cut my throat*
    Though the RAVEN, I note,
Still perched up there croaks 'Nevermore!'

* After killing myself I'll be free
  Of that pervy crap ADDISON LEE!**

** Sorry folks. That should read 'ANNABEL':
  One's a taxi and one's a dead girl...

George Büchner

Having dealt now with DICKENS and POE
We rejoin Eng. Lit's onwardly flow
    As it rushes in torrents
    From HOMER to LAWRENCE,
Though I don't now know which way to go...

We're back in the mid-1830s
I blame DICKENS whom critics assert is
    Much better than LYTTON!
    My choice, then is quittin'
Or dig to find where the paydirt is*

So come on, folks! Keep your eyes peeled
For riches our search may yet yield…
    Yes! Over there! Look! Nah...
    Yes! It's GEORGE BÜCHNER!!
Standing out in his own field!

Expressionist *avant la lettre*,
Had he lived then he'd have proved Le Maitre**
    Of Weird!! *WOYZECK*'s odd,
    But so's *DANTON'S TOD*,
LENZ, THE HESSIAN COURIER, etc***

*This Lit dearth, a sign of the times,
  Is reflected in most of my rhymes.

** A German Romantic & Mensch
  (Though phrases found here are in French)
  He died young of typhus, health wrecked,
  But thus pathed the way for BERT BRECHT!

*** And in the int'rests of my health
  I've not precis'd here. Read 'em yourself...

Heinrich Heine

a serious Limerick

Looking down from High Heaven H. HEINE
Said, 'In retrospect, please define a
    Nation who'll read a
    Book called *BUCH DER LEIDER*
In café or palace, and shine; a

People who love *eine kleine*
Musik by SCHUMANN,' said Heine,
    'We called *Dichter Lieber*.
    The great Queen of Sheba
Ne'er ruled sensibilities finer.

In Germany, France – even China –
They read me turn major keys minor!
    Yet each Romantic Lyric
    I penned then proved pyrrhic.
And because I love Freedom,' wept HEINE,

'I mocked and loathed castle and steeple
And wrote ironic love songs to keep all
    Yearning from yawning…
    They ignored my warning
And burned my books. Then they burned people...'

The Brontës

The time: 1830s; Place: Lyme,
Where the crumbling cliffs, well worth a climb,
    Reveal loads of fossils
    Who see off Apostles
In deep geological time.

And though Churchmen gibber and shout,
Insisting the Flood wiped them out,
    When God puts before us
    A Megalosaurus
These dinosaurs call all in doubt!*

But if Learning's in flux, what of Lit?
Did dinosaurs feature? A bit.
    I think no great classic
    Is all that Jurassic,
But if you look North, there's a fit.

The BRONTËS were not from a poor class
Though all could've done with some more brass
    While the moors stretched for miles
    'Cos the girls all got piles!**
And there is your link – BRONTË sore arse!***

---

*It was LYELL who made such talk legal
  While DARWIN embarked on *The Beagle*...

**The vicarage in Howarth was drafty
  (And draughty with books too! There's crafty!)

*** BRANWELL cracked this joke. 'Oh good grief!'
  The girls cried. More of them o'erleaf.

As he dipped each girl's head in the font, he
Reflected, did Reverend BRONTË,
    With his home's cold stone floors
    And the wild windswept moors
They'd never be that MARY QUANTY,

Nor would they dress in diamonte,*
Nor croon tunes like H. BELLAFONTE,
    But though they lacked looks
    These girls might write books!
And thus was the fate of each BRONTË,

So he brought them up showing you can dwell
On moors and write verse that can scan well
    While the damp, folk insist, has
    Killed Mum and two sisters
And a stoned, pissed-up brother called BRANWELL!

But you'll see there's a problem here. Hell!
The name's hard to rhyme and to spell!
    Which is why, I suppose,
    The BRONTËS all chose
As their first *nom de plume* the name BELL…**

* It's said thus in posh shops, like 'Modom'.
  And if folk don't believe me – well, sod 'em!

** Plus they said they were male. It's not sarky
  To blame this sleight on Patriarchy…

Jane Eyre

Dear Reader, my name is JANE EYRE.
No folk round these parts really care,
    For I am an Orphan
    And many a corffin
Is filled with my best friends. Despair

Is compounded when I must, perforce,
Seek Work (as a Governess, of course)
    Worse still, my new boss
    Will be terribly cross
'Cos I made him fall off of his horse!

But we fall in love! Then we get proof
That life is a bitch, for in truth,
    While we two got pally
    His first wife's doolally
And locked in a room near the roof! *

I flee! I return! Had I tarried… Him?
She burned the place down! Cruel fate harried him:
    Blind and crippled! Will no man
    In this *bildungsroman*
Be mine at last?!? Reader – I married him! **

* 'It's BIGAMY!' We plight our troth
  To these words, though it's big of us both.

** Though given his state when I married him
  In practice thereafter I carried him..

Wuthering Heights

MR LOCKWOOD, on one of those nights
Yorkshire's famous for, gets several frights!*
    Is 'e 'avin' a laff?
    'No!' his host cries. 'It's CATH!'
NELLIE DEAN explains, 'at Wuthering Heights

CATHY loved HEATHCLIFF, though wed
ED. CATH's bro HINDLEY, it's said,
    Drank. Ed's sis ISSY
    O'er HEATHCLIFF grew dizzy.
Their son LINTON's a drip. All are dead

Save HEATHCLIFF, and now he's benighted
Those two children's lives!** All is righted
    When Lockwood returns
    Eight months later and learns
H. & CATH are in Death reunited!

'But HEATHCLIFF were wild!' NELL said. 'Mothering
Is what that lad needed. Or smothering.
    But the lot – has thou guessed? –
    Were so sexually repressed***
They all needed a bloody good Wuthering!'

* A ghost, past the window, went whoosh!
  It's described very well by Kate Bush.

** HARETON, HINDLEY's son, was now, I fear
   HEATHCLIFF'S ward. And CATH's CATH's girl.All Clear?

*** Do you think – though in shame is this voiced –
   As she wrote it that EMILY got... moist?

The Tenant of Wildfell Hall

On those wild windswept moors without trees
Certain factors pertain, if you please:
    The men are Byronic
    (Though their manners are chronic)
And the BRONTË girls all come in threes!

So, the first Mrs ROCHESTER's call
Will ruin your sleep; then you'll fall
    For brooding HEATHCLIFFE!
    Then read ANNE B.'s riff
In *THE TENANT OF WILDFELL HALL*.

For herein this fem'nist debunks
Traditional marriage! She dunks
    Her women in deeper
    Than when thou dipst sheep! Er...
The men? They're adulterous drunks!

Let's rebrand the *œuvre* so it's stated
The Sisters' lives won't be frustrated!
    ROCHESTER and his mate
    Will seek help from Relate,
And HEATHCLIFFE, of course, be castrated...

The Deaths of the Brontës

When Death in his fatal chains trusses
Great writers, then moans & loud cusses
    Will greet the accurs'd!
    But worser than worst
Is when Death comes in bunches, like buses...

E. BRONTE went first. What a shame,
With just *WUTHERING HEIGHTS* to her name.
    ANN's next! *AGNES GREY*
    'S a Tetralogy! Hey,
Death gathered her in just the same.

CHARLOTTE, next on Death's List, in a sweat,
Complained, 'Your clock's fast! Don't come yet!
    You've turned up too early!
    I'm still writing *SHIRLEY*
And reading the proofs of *VILLETTE*!'

Death took her before*. What a yob.
And all we can do now is sob
    O'er their unwritten *oeuvre*,
    Lost to Death's cruel scythe's curve **
These days publishers do that job.

*Writers die of typhoid & T.B.
 Living north of N.W.3...

**Though I'd scream with my very last breath
 This rhyme proves there's Fates Worse than Death.

Macaulay

Like those sad BRONTËS, must one be poorly
To write books and poetry? Surely
   One can be Hale and Hearty
   And also be Arty!
Consider LORD THOMAS MACAULAY!

This Historian, Statesman and Poet
Had a dicky heart, though you'd not know it
   From his WHIG HISTORY, written
   When he's fighting fit 'n'
His *LAYS OF ANCIENT ROME* will show it!

'LARS PORSENA swore by nine gods
He'd sort out those smug Roman sods
   But HORATIUS blocked
   The bridge and then socked
The Tuscans and evened the odds!'

Hmmm. That signally failed to amaze.
Didn't quicken the pulse. Didn't raise
   A smile or a snicker...
   He should've been sicker!
They aren't even those kind of *lays*!*

*The age of this joke, it's been stated,
 Is known 'cos it's been carbon dated...

The Victorians

This *LIMERICKIAD* is overdue
A pause in which to form an Overview.
    Time's winds Hyperborean
    Blow us Lit Victorian!
Yet even my poor dumb dog Rover knew

To tease out an o'er-arching theme's
Not as easy as it perhaps seems.
    Lit steamed on, strength to strength,
    But VICTORIA's reign's length
Means you'll find common threads in your dreams,*

What connects Mrs OLIPHANT (piled
Up books she'd penned) with OSCAR WILDE?
    Was Lit better or gone bad,
    'Twixt MARRYAT and CONRAD?**
Not even a five year old child

Could have for one second confused
Bulk for purpose in what it perused.
    If one thing links Vic Lit
    Then *this*, Reader, is it:
QUEEN VICTORIA wasn't amused!

*Empire & Industrialisation
 I admit, in shaping the nation,
 Just about, at a push, perhaps maybe
 Link *MORTE D'ARTHUR* and a Water Baby...

** For a full list (done Dickens) from BORROW
  To ZANGWILL, please wait till tomorrow...

Browning

By Victoria's reign we were drowning
In LIT, and you'd think they were clowning
    In giving such choice!
    But hey! Let's rejoice
At this richness of talent! Take BROWNING.

And yet while he sought out renown in
His poetry surely his crownin'
    Achievement's his life
    And how he won his wife
Who lived in the smart part of town in

Wimpole Street where her Dad's frowning
While Browning just thinks of ungowning
    The sickly Ms BARRETT
    As he enters her garret:
'Let's elope to Italia!' cried BROWNING.

And sure enough soon they're both downing
Chianti in pints 'neath an awning *
    As he whispers 'Just look
    At my *RING AND THE BOOK*!'
'Just the book will do, said Mrs BROWNING**

*If you think this rhyme's off, to be sure,
 Read *SORDELLO* if you want obscure...

**Good advice, cos *LOVE AMONG THE RUINS*
 He wrote on a diet of pruins...

My Last Duchess

'See that up there? That's my last Duchess,
And usually they're much of a muchness,
    But this one was smiley,
    A fact I found highly
Suspicious, as blokes walk on crutches

If they smile back and fall in my clutches!
But that's still the dead spit of my Duchess
    Who is now deceased.
    I spoke. All smiles ceased.
Future Duchesses I'll keep in hutches.'

The Lost Leader

For a handful of silver, please note,
Plus a ribbon to stick on his coat
 He left us! Sold out!!
 What was that all about?
He slunk off with slaves, the old scrote!

Glad confident morning no more!
Our Cause backed by poets galore
 Except WILLIAM WORDSWORTH
 Who's not worth a turd's worth
Still, God will forgive him, I'm sure.

The Pied Piper of Hamelin

In Hamelin they've had their fill
Of rats!/hats!/cats!/vats!/twats! Until
    The rhymes can't get riper!
    They hire a PIED PIPER!
They should've called in Rentokil...

They don't pay the PIPER, thus authorin'
A worse fate that leaves them all sore! For in-
    Curring his wrath
    He leads all their kids off!
They really just should've tried Warfarin...

How They Brought the Good News from Ghent to Aix

I sprang to the stirrup – whoopee!
With JORIS and DIRK, and we three
      Then galloped a gallop
      (Or 'wallop', a Malop-
Ropism)! Diddly-dee!

So gallopy gallopy went
Our gallopy horses till spent!
      Dee-diddly-dum!
      Tee-tiddly-tum!!
And *that's* how the news came from Ghent!

Childe Roland to the Dark Tower Came

This cripple was lying (and lame):
Still, I went where his finger did aim:
    The landscape was grotty;
    The sky, sort of... snotty,
Which is really all rather a shame.

[*I, BROWNING, have garnered my fame*
With Poetry that draws acclaim!
    But frankly – Oh Lordy!
    This one gets quite gaudy.
Here we go now with more of the same.]

Palsied oaks, leprous lichen inflame
Disgust; the word 'life' doth defame
    Such things! It's hard copian
    With stuff this dystopian,
Like that book *THE ROAD* by Whatsisname...

As I trudged on my purpose became
Even more obscure, though I'm still game;
    [*I'll explain – BROWNING here –*
    I'm just quoting KING LEAR]
'Childe Roland to the dark tower came!'

Elizabeth Barratt Browning

We've done BROWNING though not his Mrs,
An oversight that rightly pisses
    Off a FEMINIST CRITIC
    Who, more analytic
Than me, would cry 'Read her!' and this is

Because she, sick, up in her garret,
Was solid gold, 24 carat
    And can easily outbid
    Liquorice Allsorts* or SYD
As History's most famous BARRETT

(Though Barratt Homes* come a close second –
Ignore that) for it has been reckoned
    Although she's long gone
    Her verses outshone
Her husband's, her Muse was so fecund!

'How do I love thee? Count the ways'.
That's one of hers. See how it plays
    On one's heartstrings. For sure,
    I'd just love to read more.
I'll get round to it one of these days.**

*Spelled different, I know. Don't get frantic
 I deftly defy the pedantic.

** You object? Well, I don't give a fig!
 I'm a hungover chauvinist pig...

Flush

Last page I was in such a rush
I quite forgot something! I blush,
    Coz LIZ BARRETT BROWNING
    Was famous for owning
A dear little doggie called FLUSH!'*

So let us just briefly digress
On doggies in literature! Bless!
    Like *GREYFRIARS BOBBY*
    (I'm getting all sobby)
Or ARGOS or *WHITE FANG* ** I guess

We must add to them mongrels and tikes
And vicious brutes nobody likes
    Like BASKERVILLE'S Hound
    (Which belonged in a pound)
Or BULL'S EYE, once owned by BILL SIKES,

And those curs that need medical checks
Or dry hump your leg to have sex,
    But of all Man's Best Friends
    In Lit one commends
The most that pooch 'OEDIPUS REX'!***

*Written up, in a *canidae* loop,
  By V. WOOLF, of the Bloomsbury Group.

** I'd include, though it make me a whinger,
  My own dog, our blind poodle GINGER.

*** Though I may be quite wrong about OEDIPUS,
   Which could be mis-spelling of 'Greedy Puss'...

Engels and Marx

1848: This year *PENDENNIS*
Is published, and yet greater menace
    Than 'Who wins the lady' –
    Things more…barricadey –
Stalked Europe from Berlin to Venice!

The point was: to whom go the spoils?
The Boss? Or the Worker who toils?
    As this stuff is more Chartist
    Than typical artist
It won't do to just paint in oils*.

The Bourgeoisie were a pest so
ENGELS and MARX said 'Hey Presto!
    Haunting this whole sector
    'S a great big red spectre
Says *THE COMMUNIST MANIFESTO*!

For it's clear Dialectics will juggle
The fate of each wizard** and muggle
    And where Classes slither to
    Because History Hitherto
Has been the Hist'ry of Class Struggle!'

*They sought chaps for the job near and far,
  The closest they came? Delacroix!

**Materialist magic?! Well yeah!
  How else does all melt into air?

As we've seen, MARX and ENGELS did limn
An Analysis that does not skim
    Over stuff that's quite scary –
    Revolutionary!
You know! People torn limb from limb!

And yet, placed in context, let's trim
Dialectics that make us all swim
    With History's tide;
    Just as an aside
Why not view this (unless you're too dim)

As more German Romantics who hymn
The fervid right up to the brim!
    Therefore FRIEDRICH and KARL
    (Although Marxists may snarl)
Link straight back to the – BROTHERS GRIMM!*

What?! You cry. Shhh! This does not bedim
Their achievements. But just on a whim
    Think of forests and witches
    And how Capital enriches
Capitalists and it's all – well – grim.

*Rumpelstiltskin' – this isn't contrarian –
  Was obviously proletarian!

Tennyson

Compare limericks to ALFRED LORD TENNYSON;
It's like saying spam is like venison!
    The twain cannot meet
    In poetic conceit
And shower us with golden benison!

Yet any Victorian denizen
Would wager their guineas and pennies on
    A tweak and a fiddle
    Somewhere round the middle
And Voila! We've limericked TENNYSON!

In Memoriam

In the late 1840s a bolt
From the blue in that Age of Revolt:
    A poem appears;
    Its author took years
Musing on his dead mate. *Oy gevalt*!

I mean TENNYSON's *IN MEMORIAM*
On his mate ARTHUR HALLAM whose gory jam,
    In his cranium went 'ping!'*
    And his spirit took wing
And wafted him upwards to Glory! Am

I too glib? Here's some (it's your call):
'I hold it true, whate'er befall
    When I feel sorrow most;
    Better t'have loved and lost
Than never to have loved at all.'

Oo-er missus! Here's more of his screed:
'Who trusted God was love indeed
    And love the last law
    Tho' red in tooth and claw
All Nature shriek'd against His creed!**

*In poetic terms I've a dilemma: which
   Way to say: 'Died – a brain haemorrhage'?

**With some fiddling this verse structure's fine
   As Limericks! Just add a first line!

In the off-chance that you didn't notice
ALFRED, LORD TENNYSON wrote us
    A load of more stuff!
    One life ain't enough
To read it all! *EATERS OF LOTOS*

Inspired him when he wasn't makin'
Verse about things like *THE KRAKEN*
    (Or possibly Kraken)
    And please, reader, harken
To *ULYSSES*! ALF wasn't fakin'!

And thanks to things like *MARIANA*
He proved that he was top banana
    Though he spent decades fiddling
    With the King's idylling
'Is it done yet?' they cried. He: '¡*Mañana*!'

So charge up your glasses! Hoorah!
To ALFRED, LORD TENNYSON! Star
    And great Poet Laureate!
    More drinks, barman! *Floreat*!
Where are those drinks? Crossing the bar!

The Lady of Shalott

She left the web, she left the loom,
She made three paces thro' the room
    When SIR LANCELOT
    Trotted from Camelot;
She saw the helmet and the plume.

Out flew the web and floated wide;
The mirror crack'd from side to side
    When the DAME OF SHALOTT
    Saw SIR LANCELOT!
'The curse is... upon me!' she cried.*

*Plus she damned poor Cliff Richard to Hell
And was 'half sick of Shadows' as well.

Maud

'Come into the garden now MAUD!'
(Hot diggedy! Think I've just scored!)
   'For the black bat night's flown!'
   (Now I'll rip off her gown*
Oh shit! I'm Victorian! Gaaawd...)

*These pronunciations are all echt
 Victorian archaic. I've checked.

Blow Bugle Blow

Blow bugle blow! Set echoes flying,
The horns of Elfland dy-dy-dying !
   Blow! Hark! Are they vying
   With far glens replying?
If you say you like this stuff, you're lying.

The Charge of the Light Brigade

Half a league onwards they thundered
Into the Valley! Six hundred
    Rode half a league further!
    What happens next's Murther!*
And many folks reading this wondered

How, after the generals had blundered,
TENNYSON thereafter plundered
    His skills to make gory
    Incompetence glory!
(His Muses all therafter chundered...)

*This archaic spelling's a hoot! Gloat
Once more over page 90's footnote!

The Pre-Raphaelites

TENNYSON, all knew, was gloomy;
His verse made VICTORIA's eyes rheumy!
    But that's how you get
    To be Laureate!
If you doubt my analysis sue me!

Meanwhile, 'midst 1848's
Revolutions a louche bunch of mates
    Replaced workers' anger
    With Epicene langour
Amongst other similar traits

Like knocking out stuff really trippy
Like some kind of prototype Hippy!
    So let us acquaint us
    With Poets & Painters
Who were so incredibly drippy!

(No, really. Of things you should smother, would
You choose, apple pie, say or Motherhood?
    Oh no. It's boys willowy
    Who need a fate pillowy!)
I present the Pre-Raphaelite Brotherhood!

The Pre-Raphaelite bruvs were 'Pathetic!'
Some said; others said 'Diuretic!'
    'Nitpickingly anal!'
    'Archaic!' 'Banal!'*
Yet they forged the Victorian aesthetic!

And when modelling for the Pre-Raphs
You must lie round for hours in cold baths
    While JOHN EV'RETT MILLAIS
    Paints *OPHELIA* all day.
And have a neck like a giraffe's,

And hair thick and lush, like LIZ SIDDAL
Whose death, to this day, is a riddle.
    (Then ROSSETTI, now Randy
    On chloral and brandy
Gave JANE MORRIS's tresses a fiddle!)

Plus you'll need a cow's large, liquid eye
And the morals of sows in a sty
    And lips full and scarlet!
    'Sides from that, any harlot
Or anyone else could apply!

*If this seems odd let me acquaint us
 With RUSKIN's stress, in *MODERN PAINTERS.*

The Pre-Raphaelites weren't all just painting
Young women who look like they're fainting.
    It gets even worse:
    They also wrote verse,
Equally or yet more unrestraint-ing!

For DANTE GABRIEL ROSSETTI
Wrote poems (increasingly sweaty)
    About Love & Death
    While he took Crystal Meth*
And MORRIS, who looked like a yeti,

As he sat by the light of a taper
Said 'I'll have a bash at this verse caper!'
    So he did, and upon
    My soul, it goes on
And on, like a role of wallpaper!**

And when R's wife croaked he like a berk,
Lay some verse 'side her corpse! Didn't shirk
    Poor LIZ to exhume
    To fill a volume
With the whole of his *body* of work!***

*It was chloral & Brandy he sniffed
 In reality – you get my drift...

**Believe me: costs more than a tanner
  To wallpaper all Kelmscott Manor!

*** By now he was fat as a porpoise.
     If you want to, please read 'work' as 'corpus'.

Christina Rossetti

D. G. ROSSETTI's demeanour
When writing verse could've been cleaner
    Instead he just leered
    And generally appeared
Quite unlike his sister CHRISTINA

Who was pious, poetic and chaste
(Her bro just chased chicks and disgraced
    Himself. Oh so 'Fleshy'
    His poems were; 'Meshy'*
His sheets, which were seldom replaced.)

Nonetheless her out-put lights the dark; it
Spreads in a poetical arc; it
    Goes from *IN THE BLEAK*
    MIDWINTER to streak
All the way over to *GOBLIN MARKET*

In which we find CHRISTINA cobblin'
Temptation to Gender, thus wobblin'
    Quite perilously near
    To her bro's stuff! I hear
Though that he preferred messier gobblin'...

*His various sexual adventures
  Required he be fitted with dentures...

Swinburne

In ROSSETTI's gang lurk chaps whose kin yearn
Will, thanks to the depths of their sin, burn
    In Hell 'cos they're decadent!
    Live lives that can wreck a gent!*
Like ALGERNON CHARLIE SWINBURNE!

Dirty minded and drunk, Verse refines
His life! Yet through Drink he declines
    Till he just lies there gruntin'...
    Then THEODORE WATTS DUNTON*
Dried him out in Putney in 'The Pines.'

There are others hung out with or sat for
The Pre-Raphs, and solely on that score
    Are remembered today
    For their writing too! Hey!
For example, there's COVENTRY PATMORE**

Or GEORGE MEREDITH, who had it rough;
Posed for 'The Death of CHATTERTON'; Tough
    That, painted from Life,
    Painter then nicked his wife!
Didn't happen to ARTHUR HUGH CLOUGH...***

*Weak rhymes like this can come in handy
 Ripped to yer tits on dope and brandy!

**Neither decadent nor that notorious
  C PATMORE *was* deeply uxorious...

*** M. wrote *MODERN LOVE* when his marriage faileth;
   C wrote 'Say Not The Struggle Naught Availeth.'

Thackeray

Having started off writing pure hackery
And moving on to Paddy-Whackery
    (That's in *BARRY LYNDON*,
    A rascal who sinned) 'n'
Avoiding DICKENS' Christmas-crackery

And mawkishness, how much more blacker he
Depicted Mankind, stripped of lacquerie,
    In books like *PENDENNIS*
    Throughout which his pen is
Employed exposing snobbish slackery

That yearns for more unearned Knick-Knackery
By cynically seeking a backer (he
    Is rich, like R. DESMOND –
    Or a King in '*H. ESMOND*')
Whether he be a young laddish Jack or he

Is really a she, and a cracker! She
Is so wicked why don't they thwack her? Be
    Calm. Have a chair.
    Next up's *VANITY FAIR*!
Otherwise, that's the novels of THACKERAY.

Vanity Fair

In *VANITY FAIR* there's no hero
So don't expect one to appear! Though
    AMELIA's quite nice
    BECKY SHARP's steeped in vice
And her prospects of improvement zero!

Yet she seeks through the book to be boss!
Tries – and ends nabbing – A's fat bro JOS;
    Eyes the CRAWLEYs – PITT, RAWDON
    (Gets R); then the bawd on
A's hubby GEORGE* preys! A. gets cross...

Then before Waterloo there's a Ball
And next day GEORGE gets killed! (All in all
    George was vile.) A's so vapid
    Her fall is now rapid:
Sad & poor, now disowned, she must crawl

To dead GEORGE's Dad, who's a pain,
Like the rest. (BECK's** off porking LORD STEYN)
    While poor faithful DOBBIN
    Does not get his knob in
Till the book's nearly over! Insane!

*George OSBORNE's his name! It's engrossin'
  His spoilt son's lackey's called ROWSON!

**Although I do not wish carp
  The best character's clearly Ms SHARP!

Carlyle

At its height the Victorian Age is
Replete with books whose many pages
    Are full up to show it's
    Got Authors & Poets
And more than its fair share of Sages.

For starters there's THOMAS CARLYLE
Who railed 'gainst the Modern World while
    He bigged up The Hero
    Which is rather queer though
It explains why he never did smile,

Though his life with his wife was quite brusque. In
Their Chelsea Home, reeking of musk, in
    This marriage, it's said,
    They both wished they were dead!
Wedded Bliss got much worse for JOHN RUSKIN

Who'd been brought up amid great art's splendour,
So when his wife he did upend 'er
    He recoiled in dismay
    For no lady in, say,
RAPHAEL had such hairy pudenda!*

*Do not fear – in the end she's OK
  Once she's run off with JOHNNY MILLAIS...

Matthew Arnold

Wives apart, RUSKIN & T. CARLYLE
Berated the Public in style!
    RUSKIN would acquaint us
    With exactly which painters
We all should disparage. Meanwhile

He wrote *CROWN OF WILD OLIVE* (a blast!);
Even more fun was *UNTO THIS LAST*;
    While CARLYLE scorned the basest
    And got kinda racist...
But we've left someone out of this cast:

MATTHEW ARNOLD's languorous cool gaze
Surveyed The Age up, down and all ways,
    So when folk got panicky
    He wrote *CULTURE AND ANARCHY*
(His father inspired *TOM BROWN'S SCHOOLDAYS*).

He also composed *DOVER BEACH*
Which goes: 'Does Mankind overreach?
    The Tide's going out
    So all's called in doubt!
Let's build a sandcastle! That's peach!'*

*I concede that my precis's bereft
 Of some teleological heft...

102

Brunel

It's really not nuclear fission
To notice a massive omission
    In Victorian Lit
    For nobody writ
Great Lit on the Great Exhibition!

This is simply down to arty malice
From bards who thought the crystal palace
    Was all about Trade
    And oiks (all self made)
To whom they would not raise a chalice.*

But take ISAMBARD KINGDOM BRUNEL,
A mere engineer! But he knew well
    There's more poetry in steam
    Than at first there might seem
As each train thundered through a fresh tunel!

I'm sorry. That should've read 'tunnel' –
It rhymes with the Great Eastern's funnel.
    So those bards had a point:
    No poet can anoint
Isambard till his name's changed to BRUNNEL.

*The problem is, poets are snobs
 Who've never held down proper jobs.

North and South

Although it was unsung in fiction
Hoorah for the Great Exhibiction!*
    Thrived through word of mouth
    Though betwixt North and South
There were regional changes in diction.

Bluff Millowners who thought that soup
Slurped with a spoon proved them up
    In the world thought it 'Class!'
    'Cos it made loads of brass!
In the South, though, they said 'Can't recoup

With cesh any leck of good breedin' '
It was true! Simply check what they're reading!
    In the South they loved prose
    While up North it was rows
Of numbers in ledgers, thus leading

To Cultural Fissures. Yet ask all
Parties to answer the task: all
    Concur, South or North
    And cry 'Jast baagah orff!'
'Ay lad! Go and ask Mrs GASKELL!'

*In Kensington we know this reads
  As skewiff, but not up in Leeds...

George Borrow

1851 still must detain us,*
For Lit thundered on. This was heinous.
    MRS GASKELL wrote *CRANFORD*
    Though this cunning plan would
Mean TV Gold would entertain us!

Then there's GEORGE BORROW's book *LAVENGRO*,
At the sight of which critics cried 'Whoa!'
    And then they attacked!
    Was it fiction or fact?
Don't ask me! How on earth should I know?**

Having said that this much remains clear:
If you go to a library quite near
    And say, 'Can I borrow
    This book?' 'Call tomorrow,'
They'll say, 'and you'll find it's still here.'

If all of this makes you feel sick
Look for LIT o'er the wide Atlantic!
    THE HOUSE OF SEVEN GABLES
    Saw the Yanks turn the tables,
And a sight – at least – of (MOBY) DICK!***

*Readers had made the admission:
 'We're sick of the Great Exhibition!'

** I sing thee of Lit! Bloody Hell!
  Do you want me to read it as well?!?

*** The Puritan Legacy'll mean
    That, apart from this, I'll keep it clean .

Hawthorne

If you don't want a Lit that's all forlorn*
You'll be needing someone to pour scorn
    On your National Psyche,
    Yet big it up! Crikey!
Step forward NATHANIEL HAWTHORNE!

For nobody could've shown better
Than Nat did in his *SCARLET LETTER*
    The Yanks up to the hilt
    In Puritan Guilt
Which they wore like a thick iron fetter.

The Plot? Boston Town's HESTER PRYNNE
Wears a Scarlet 'A' (denotes her Sin)
    Because the local vicar's
    Been inside her knickers!**
He confesses at last and dies. Fin.

Life wouldn't've been such a wrench
If they'd just used a letter... that's French
    And made out of rubber.
    Next page we hunt blubber
Just off the Mariana Trench...

*If you're pained by this over-reached scansion
  It matches the US's expansion
  Either Westward to the Shining Sea
  Or beyond the bounds of Poetry...

**The result of this union is PEARL,
  A child who would make DICKENS hurl...

Moby Dick

[*The book starts like this*] Call me ISHMAEL
And I sailed o'er the seas full of fish! Hail
   My new friend QUEEQUEG
   A savage I'd beg
Is better than white men I'd wish jail!

We set sail aboard *The Pequod*
Whose captain was extremely odd,
   For a whale, out at sea,
   Ate his leg 'neath the knee
While leaving the rest of his bod.

The mad captain was name of AHAB
Sans whose idée fixe life would stay drab
   'I will be revenged!
   He cries! (He's unhenged*
And should've tried sticking with rehab*).

But, if you deplore his whole shtick
Relax, cos it's all symbolic
   Er... well, I guess... erm...
   Um... We know the whale's sperm
So that why he's called MOBY DICK**!

*They pronounced things like this in Nantucket
 And if you don't like it, well...

** If this cheapening smut boils your blood,
 Cf the end of *BILLY BUDD*.

Melville

MELVILLE's oeuvre, it has to be said,
In his lifetime was largely unread,
    MOBY DICK was too weird
    And the critics all feared
That Melville had gone off his head.*

Published posthumously, *BILLY BUDD*
Was abandoned by MELVILLE. 'It's crud!'
    He cried, so it's queer
    BRITTEN helped make it clear
That it's actually frightfully good!**

Then there's *BARTLEBY THE SCRIVENER*
About a weird clerk who is given a
    Job he won't do!
    'I choose not to.' 'Boo hoo!'
Weeps his boss who is driven to within a

Ninch of despair by that BARTLEBY!
Yet here MELVILLE shows us what part he'll be
    Given by Lit!
    He pre-empts, by a bit,
The Modern, so shows us what art'll be!

*This is sad, because his book *TYPEE*
 Had made critics should out 'Yippee!'

**BEN pronounced this word thus, if one checks,
  Then wrote 'Clear seamen from the decks!'

Thoreau

'Taxing governments, oh how I hate ya!'
Cried HENRY THOREAU, 'so it's great ya
    Don't need slugs of JAMESON,
    Just RALPH WALDO EMERSON*
And his uplifting volume called *NATURE*

To make one move to Walden Pond,
'Neath the palms** and each green bosky frond!
    The view? What a charmer!
    EMERSON, LAKE and PALM! Er...***
And all in the back of beyond!'

But hold it right there, Henry Thoreau,
And look to years beyond tomorrow:
    Whereas you're arty-farty,
    They'll form the Tea Party,
A cause for considerable sorrow!

And Life in the Woods, I declare,
In a vast open toilet for bear?
    It's not 'Disobedience'!
    It's simple expedience
To decide that you're not going there!

*If this rhyme strikes you as quite mentalist
  Relax! It is just Transcendentalist!

**For the Latitude palm trees, I know
  Are wrong. Cf this gag below. ***

*** I know this may come as a shock
   But these Yankees all worshipped Prog Rock!

Harriet Beecher Stowe

In the wood HENRY THOREAU was grabbin'
Some rays by his hut, idly dabbin'
    Suntan lotion galore
    On his bonce, while next door...*
Good heavens! It's *UNCLE TOM'S CABIN*!

This eponymous humble slave's dwelling
Became internationally bestselling!
    Sales like TOPSY did grow
    Because H. BEECHER STOWE
Told a tale worth repeated retelling!

And despite racial stereotyping
This book very soon helped in wiping
    Out Slavery! Cor!
    Plus a whole civil war!
Few novels get that kind of hyping!

Tom's hut's location, nonetheless,
To this day remains anyone's guess.
    No.1 Catfish Row?
    Possibly, but I know
That that's not the Gettysburg address!

*Not literally, you daft twit,
But in the canon of Yank Lit.
And though you may find this fact scary:
Next to that's *LITTLE HOUSE ON THE PRAIRIE*!

Hiawatha

If a publisher made you an offer
Guaranteed to fill up a large coffer
    Would you write about slaves
    Or about Indian braves,
UNCLE TOM'S CABIN or *HIAWATHA*?

Neither was penned by an amateur,
Though *TOM* pushes out Lit's parameter,*
    As 'twas written in Wrath,
    Unlike *HIAWATH-***
A, writ in trochaic tetrameter.

'By the shores of Gitche Gumee,
By Giche Gumee's shoreside gloomy
    By that gloomy shore am
    By that shore a wigwam
A wigwam beside far Gitche Gumee

Stood a wood by Gitche Gumee's shore
With a wigwam upon the wood's floor
    Wood, wigwam, shore sat
    Wigwam, shore, wood...' That
Is enough. I can't stand anymore.

* Caused the Civil War, yet no one's sworn,
  HIAWATHA caused Little Big Horn.

** If you think that this messes with text
  Just wait till you see what comes next...

Whitman

Hiawatha stood baring his arse
As savages do. Let it pass,
    Because far from mental
    (Because transcendental)
Was WALT WHITMAN's book *LEAVES OF GRASS*.

His publisher sighed. 'Look here, Whitman,
These poems are basically shit, man!
    They're all 'me me me!'
    And the verse is too free!
Change them!' 'NO' 'Then I'm calling a hitman!'

The hitman arrived. 'Dese are shocking!
I don't see no readers come flocking!
    And dis *SONG OF MYSELF*
    Could prove bad for your health
While *OUT OF THE CRADLE ENDLESSLY ROCKING**

Is so contemptuous of da metric
It could prove fatal if you might get sick...'
    WALT called the cops! Yeah!
    And the hood got the chair!
And WALT sang the body electric!

*WALT WHITMAN did not even try
 To make this line scan. Why should I?

Dumas *Père*

If you view WHITMAN's scansion askance
Then reader, please avert your glance
    Across the Atlantic,
    From Yanks getting frantic
To what they were up to in France.

As lithe and as sleek as a puma
With a backlist that grew like a tumour
    (Plays! Novels! Here's looking
    At his *DICTIONARY OF COOKING*!)
I give you ALEXANDRE DUMAS!

His output's prodigious. One fears
Having got through *THE THREE MUSKETEERS*,
    THE COUNT OF MONTE CRISTO *
    Will damage your wrist! Oh!
Read fast 'fore his next book appears!

But while DUMAS wrote without cease
He treated the chicks with caprice,
    So his mistresses brooded**
    But his output included
On top of the books, DUMAS *fils*!

*The stress here might rightly appal,
  But hey! All for one, one for all!

** DUMAS *père*, all in all, was quite naughty,
  His adulteries numbering 40!

Dumas *Fils*

The young ALEXANDRE DUMAS*
Said of his famous old pa
    'He wrote of D'ARTAGNAN
    And his every companion
And their goings-on in the boudoir,

And close up or viewed from afar
I admit that my dear old papa
    Knocked out as his œuvre
    Enough stuff to prove
That he was a genuine star!

So how can I therefore crowbar
Myself onto Great Lit's radar?
    I know! 'Til midnight
    I'll stay up and write
LA DAME AUX CAMÉLIAS!

And that's how the younger DUMAS
Became the equal of his da,
    'Cos just as a starter
    It sired *LA TRAVIATA*
Which raked in the cash! Hip hurrah!!

*I don't mean the nephew or niece
 But the son, aka DUMAS, *fils*...

Some More French Novelists

Don't think DUMAS, *père ou fils*, had sewn
Up French Literature as their own.
    On top of V. HUGO
    There's more than a few go
On writing fingers to the bone!

Just think of THÈOPHILE GAUTIER,
Or CHATEAUBRIAND, who was haughtier*
    Or MÉRIMÉE's charmin'
    Novel called *CARMEN***
Which was, perforce, also much naughtier.

Nor should we leave out GEORGE SAND
This cross-dressing chain-smoker planned
    To spend her life copin'
    With consumptive CHOPIN
But then it all got out of hand.

So if you want books, these French wrote 'em!
They wrote so many books I can't quote 'em!
    While BALZAC's persistence
    Captured All Existence
And his name is translated as scrotum!***

*We're not dealing here with Lit Kraut
  So use a French Accent throughout...

**'It's obscene!' the petit-bourgeoisie say,
   'But at least it keeps MÉRIMÉE BIZET!'

*** You may find this line too much, but
   The Whole of Real Life includes smut!

Gustave Flaubert

The first novel by GUSTAVE FLAUBERT
Sought, with Realism to show where
    Romance in the Bourgeois
    Can go far far too far,
So it's best, reader, if you don't go there.

It concerns a dim doctor. CHARLES BOVARY's
Sure that he'll live life in clover! He's
    Widowed; weds EMMA
    And she is a gem! A-
Las she has got itchy ovaries,

So her love life thereafter's heartrending*;
Thrice jilted she starts overspending
    So gets sucked into Debt
    And Despair. You can bet
What you like there'll be no happy ending.**

As she dies she cries: 'This fact may shock:
I was bored by that provincial doc!
    Passion heaved in my bust
    And to use *le mot juste*
I basically wanted some coq!'***

*'Tween LEON & BOULANGER she twists
  In too many clandestine trysts...

** What is it makes chicks of her class flick
  From 'cute ass' to gobbling arsenic?!

*** Poor Emma may be oversexed
    But this is a classic French text!

Baudelaire

The French poet CHARLES BAUDELAIRE
Was anything other than square
    As he said to his readers
    'Now listen, you bleeders, –
Hypocrite lecteur – mon frère! –

Life is just squalid, you see,
And shot through with seams of *ennui*!
    In short, it's a bitch,
    Though my poetry's rich!
De dum diddle dum diddle dee!'

This attitude led to some quarrels.
He got nicked, out-raging public morals,
    Which led to a fine
    And an unwholesome shine
On his already poisonous laurels.

Everyone from Montparnasse to Dyfed's
Read BAUDY's ballads for spliff kids,
    But a warning word, pal:
    *LES FLEURS DU MAL**
Ain't a bit like *THE DAY OF THE TRIFFIDS*...

*This translates (and this took me hours)
  As something like 'Those Naughty Flowers'.

The readers of verse by CHARLES BAUDELAIRE
Are often young dudes *à la mode*, aware
    Of how cool, it is said,
    'Tis to yawn and drop dead
In a pool of your puke in the road! Oh yeah!

And hepcats in an upstairs abode declare
(Though ev'ry last one's a freeloader): 'Where
    The absinthe is drunk
    So am I, as a skunk,
And all thanks to reading CHARLES BAUDELAIRE!'

(Doctors with heavy caseload prepare
When visiting sick fans of BAUDELAIRE,
    To use camphor, not brooms,
    To sanitise their rooms
Because of the sweet foetid odour there.)

And yet, in the end, when they know despair
Guides their hands to a gun (a frontloader) they're
    Reciting refrains
    As they blow out their brains,
Composed long ago by CHARLES BAUDELAIRE!

Say It
With Flowers!

To be continued...